Give Me Your Heart

40 Devotions for the Season of Lent

DR. STEVEN BELL
REV. MEREDITH BELL
REV. CHANDLER RAGLAND

ISBN: 1519509111
ISBN 13: 9781519509116
Library of Congress Control Number: 2015919856
CreateSpace Independent Publishing Platform
North Charleston, South Carolina

TABLE OF CONTENTS

INTRODUCTION

"Be careful that you don't practice your religion in front of people to draw their attention. If you do, you will have no reward from your Father who is in heaven. Whenever you give to the poor, don't blow your trumpet as the hypocrites do in the synagogues and in the streets so that they may get praise from people. I assure you, that's the only reward they'll get. But when you give to the poor, don't let your left hand know what your right hand is doing so that you may give to the poor in secret. Your Father who sees what you do in secret will reward you. When you pray, don't be like hypocrites. They love to pray standing in the synagogues and on the street corners so that people will see them. I assure you, that's the only reward they'll get. But when you pray, go to your room, shut the door, and pray to your Father who is present in that secret place. Your Father who sees what you do in secret will reward you." (Matthew 6:1-6 CEB)

The purpose of *Give Me Your Heart* is to highlight and help you experience a powerful time in the Christian year: the season of Lent. Now, what is "Lent?" Is Lent that stuff in your dryer (or belly button!)? No, that's "lint." Lent is a season of forty days, not counting Sundays, which begins Ash Wednesday and ends the Saturday before Easter Sunday. Lent comes from an ancient word meaning, "spring." The season is a special time of preparation for celebrating Jesus' triumphant resurrection from the dead—Easter. "Historically, Lent began as a period of fasting and preparation for baptism by converts to the Christian faith, and then became a time for penance by all Christians" (*The United Methodist Book of Worship*, Nashville: The United Methodist Publishing House, 1992, pg. 320).

During Lent we are reminded of Jesus' fasting in the desert for forty days, being tempted by the devil, his suffering, and his death that brings us eternal salvation. A wonderful article entitled "Why Lent" states, Easter "is so much brighter when you have been through the darkness. To see the light of Jesus Christ's resurrection on Easter, you have to acknowledge the suffering of his execution that precedes it" (www.ministrymatters.com/all/entry/886/why-lent).

During Lent, people oftentimes give up something they like (such as coffee, Cokes, or sweets), a vice (negativity or gossip), or instead of giving up something, they add something to their daily life (daily Bible or devotional reading, prayer, random acts of kindness). However, as Jesus tells us in Matthew 6, the point of a Lenten discipline is not to show others how spiritually superior we are, but rather to prepare ourselves for the joy and celebration of Easter. It's a time of intentional faith formation. It's a season to connect with God in a powerful way. It's a series of moments when we are reminded of God's faithful call to "Give me your heart" (Joel 2:12).

Give Me Your Heart can be used for personal study and devotion as you move though the forty days of Lent towards the cross and empty tomb. It can also be used for small group study, and we have included a study guide in the back that can help focus and facilitate your group discussions when you gather together each week. Also, all proceeds of this Lenten devotion will go to a very worthy cause – Habitat for Humanity, an organization near and dear to our hearts.

We pray you and your family all experience a holy Lent this year, and it is our desire that these forty devotions will assist you in that endeavor!

Grace and Peace,

Dr. Steven Bell
Rev. Meredith Bell
Rev. Chandler Ragland

DAY 1

ASH WEDNESDAY: CLEAN HEARTS, RIGHT SPIRITS

Scripture Reference – Psalm 51:1 to 17

Devotion:
God looks on all of his people with love and tenderness. God's heart breaks when we turn away from that love through our sins and our transgressions. King David broke God's heart when he looked on Bathsheba and took her as his own, even when she was married to another. God could've left David in his sin. The Almighty could have brought down punishment from on high. But our God is a redeemer. Our God is a forgiver. The Lord doesn't want us to be broken and punished. God wants us to be purified and holy. And so we have been given the gift of repentance. David cries out when he realized the depth of his sin: "Create in me a clean heart, O God, and put a new and right spirit within me" (Psalm 51:10). And God did.

None of us are perfect. We are all marred by sin. But our Lord has no desire to leave us there. Our God is never done with us. Our redeemer wants to grow us and to mold us and to teach us what it means to follow Jesus. God wants our hearts to be clean and our spirits to be pure. That

journey towards righteousness starts with repentance. We should pray as
David prayed, "Have mercy on me, O God, according to your steadfast
love; according to your abundant mercy blot out my transgression. Wash
me thoroughly from my iniquity, and cleanse me from my sin" (Psalm 51:1
to 2). And God will do that... over and over again.

What is holding you back from righteousness? Are you afraid of God's
judgement? Or do you trust in his mercy and love?

Prayer:
Great Redeemer and Forgiver, you came and dwelled among us, not to
judge as unworthy, but to show us the path righteousness. Make my heart
clean. Make my spirit pure. I am thankful for your unending grace and
love this day and every day. Amen.

DAY 2

Scripture Reference – Acts 7:30 to 34

Devotion:
St. Stephen is known as the first Christian martyr. He was stoned to death because he was charged with blasphemy by Jewish authorities. Before his death, he delivered a long speech captured in the book of Acts about the work of God through history.

It is a moving speech. It is easy to feel the passion and truth in the words. I imagine St. Stephen was reminding himself of God's power and might just as much as he wanted to share the words with others around him. I am sure they brought comfort to him as he prepared for his death. I am sure it brought fear and wonder to those who heard his words for the first time.

We need moments in our lives where we stop and listen to God. Moments where God gets our attention and we turn our eyes away from our lives and focus them back on God. Moses experienced the best moment. He met God through a burning bush. In verse 32, God introduces himself to Moses by using his credentials; God of your ancestors, God of Abraham, Isaac and Jacob. Moses simply responds, "Trembling with fear, Moses didn't dare to investigate any further."

Many times over the years I have heard myself saying, "If only I would get a burning bush like Moses. Then I would know what I needed to do." I have heard others share similar desires. But what I am really asking for when I say these words is, "I really need to know God is near me today." St. Stephen knew God was near him because at the end of his speech, Scripture says God gave him a glimpse into heaven with God and Jesus together. Moses knew God was near because the moment together was holy.

How do you know when God is near? When was the last time you felt God's presence?

Prayer:
Today, send me a person or an experience to remind me just how near you are to me, God. Thank you for your faithfulness. Help me today adjust my eyes away from me and focus them on you. Amen.

DAY 3

FRIDAY: REFUSING GOOD NEWS

Scripture Reference – Exodus 6:1 to 13

Devotion:

God wants the hearts of his chosen ones, the Israelites. In order to take hold of their hearts, and liberate them from slavery in Egypt, God sends Moses to speak to them and free them. God instructs Moses to be his voice, and to say to the imprisoned Israelites, "I am the Lord. I will free you from your oppression and will rescue you from your slavery in Egypt. I will redeem you with a powerful arm and great acts of judgment. I will claim you as my own people, and I will be your God. Then you will know that I am the Lord your God who has freed you from your oppression in Egypt" (Exodus 6:6 and 7). Moses indeed communicates this great message to the enslaved Israelites, but they refuse to believe him. They are too discouraged to hear this good news. God then tells Moses to give Pharaoh a message: "Let my people go!" But this time Moses refuses, saying, "My own people won't listen to me anymore. How can I expect Pharaoh to listen?" (Exodus 6:12).

Throughout history, God has sought to soften the hardened heart. God's desire is that wandering hearts return to him. Sadly, our desire and practice is often the opposite. We harden our hearts. We hide our hearts from one another, and from the One with whom our hearts desire to be united – almighty God. Saint Bernard of Clairvaux, a French monk born in 1090AD, commented, "God removes the sin of the one who makes the humble confession, and thereby the devil loses the sovereignty he had gained over the human heart." We don't want the devil to have sovereignty of our heart, but rather God.

How are you hardening your heart toward the Lord? In what ways are you refusing to hear the good news that God has for you this day? Is there something Christ is calling you to do, yet you find yourself hesitating? Is there something you need to confess to God?

Prayer:
Almighty God, help me to have a heart that is open and ready to listen, hear, and respond to your Word. Speak your good news to me this day. I will believe it, and I will not refuse to heed your calling. I confess anything hardening my heart towards you. In Jesus' holy name I pray. Amen.

DAY 4

SATURDAY: WHAT TIME IS IT?

Scripture Reference – Ecclesiastes 3:1 to 8

Devotion:

King Solomon is known for his wisdom. God granted it to him in 1 Kings when he asked for an understanding mind and a discerning spirit over wealth and power (1 Kings 3:1 to 15). Solomon let that wisdom govern his own life, but he also passed it down to all the generations after him. He's credited with writing Proverbs, The Song of Solomon, and Ecclesiastes. All three of these are rightfully labeled as Wisdom Literature. His words can give us insight and direction. They can teach us to be more discerning, and they can help guide us in our everyday walk of faith. Solomon's wisdom has inspired countless people across centuries.

One of my favorite pieces inspired by him might just be "Hymn of Promise." Natalie Sleeth wrote that hymn in 1986, and I have no doubt these words of Solomon were on her heart and mind: "For everything there is a season, and a time for every matter under heaven" (Ecclesiastes 3:1). Here is the last verse of her hymn: "In our end is our beginning; in our time, infinity; in our doubt there is believing; in our life, eternity. In our death, a resurrection; at the last, a victory, unrevealed until its season, something God alone can see" (*The United Methodist Hymnal*, 707).

Sometimes we take our time for granted. Sometimes we waste it away. But God has given us this life, and God has invited us to fill it with experiences. We get to experience joy and thankfulness and hope. And sometimes we have to experience pain and loss and sadness. God is there beside us in all of it. God is there in every season of our lives, working to bring life and love. From birth to death to life after death, our Lord is there to guide us to eternal victory.

Where do you see God in your life right now? Where have you seen God in the past? How has God been there for you all along to get you to where you are right now?

Prayer:
Lord, you never leave me or forsake me. In all seasons, you are there to sustain me. For this I give you thanks. Help me to recognize your presence in my life so that I may be even more thankful for your unending grace and love. Amen.

DAY 5

MONDAY: PRIDE

Scripture Reference – 1 Chronicles 21:1 to 17

Devotion:
Pride. It is a character trait that is either good or bad. It is good in the sense of taking care of your home or how you wear your clothes. It is bad when it leads to arrogance or the feeling of superiority. It is good if it leads you to successful achievements and bad if it leads you to achievements that control your treatment of others.

King David let his pride turn from good to bad. He stepped away from God, just to experience what it might feel like to be God. His request to know the strength of his kingdom could have been innocent if it wasn't covered with his pride. He wanted to know simply because he wanted to feel the power he possessed. This request led him back to God who showed his power and mercy.

Carl Jung says, "Through pride we are ever deceiving ourselves. But deep down below the surface of the average conscience a still, small voice says to us, something is out of tune." Lent is a season for us to find that something (or somethings) that are out of tune. It is a season where we feel God's judgment and God's mercy. It is a season that leads us to the cross to remind us of the power of repentance and forgiveness.

How has your pride led you away from God over the past year? As you turn back to God, what changes do you feel need to be made?

Prayer:
Forgive me, God, where I have sinned and put my desires ahead of yours. Fill me with your guidance and grace as I strive to live according to your holy Word. Amen.

DAY 6

TUESDAY: SNATCHED FROM THE FIRE

Scripture Reference – Zechariah 3:1 to 10

Devotion:

A few weeks ago, a new friend of mine asked me what I do for fun. After thinking for a few moments, I realized I do a whole lot of things for fun. I run. I fish. I hunt. I play with my children. I spend time with my wife. And I camp. I love to camp. I love to camp with my family, with friends, and alone. Camping, especially when you get to camp for multiple days, is a great way to spend quality time outdoors. One of my favorite things about camping is the campfire, and one of my favorite things about the campfire is roasting marshmallows. I'll usually eat only one or two, but I love to roast them – and I've got it down to a science. I don't like my marshmallows burnt, but I also don't like them undercooked (because you can get worms from undercooked marshmallows, right!). So I slowly roast them high over the coals until they become a perfectly toasted brown delicacy. The only drawback to this technique is that you have a potential for the gooey treat to slide off your stick into the fire – and once it's in the fire, it's gone (and you have to start all over). There is no retrieving a wayward marshmallow from the fire.

But Zechariah 3 tells of something (someone) who was snatched from the fire. This someone was the high priest Joshua. Joshua had been accused by Satan. He was like a marshmallow burning up amongst the flames and coals of a campfire, because of his own sin. But that's not the end of the story. God saves him from Satan (and saves him from sin). Because of his love for Joshua, God rebukes Satan, his tricks, his schemes, and does what otherwise couldn't be done – he snatches Joshua from the fire.

Not only does God save the high priest, but he also instructs Joshua to, "follow my ways and carefully serve me." It's one thing to confess God's sovereignty verbally. It's one thing to confess with our LIPS that Jesus is Lord (Romans 10:9). It's quite another thing to confess with our LIVES that God is sovereign and Jesus is Lord. God wants our faith in him to be both verbal and behavioral. He wants our belief in him to be real and from the heart. God wants us to confess with our lips that Jesus is Lord, believe in our hearts that God raised him from the dead, follow his ways, and carefully serve him. That is the picture of a life that has been saved. That's the picture of a life that has been snatched from the fire.

Are you following God's ways, and carefully serving God? How would you say you are doing this? Is faith in Jesus something you only confess with your lips, or do you also live your faith out with your life? How has God snatched you from the fire?

Prayer:
Almighty God, to you in private and public I confess with my lips that Jesus is Lord. I believe in my heart that you raised him from the dead. I will follow your ways and carefully serve you all the days of my life. Thank you for this blessed salvation. Thank you for snatching me from the fire. In Jesus' name I pray. Amen.

DAY 7

WEDNESDAY: RESILIENT FAITHFULNESS

Scripture Reference – Job 1:1 to 22

Devotion:
We know the story of Job because of the great loss that he suffered in his life. We know it because it's the one place in the whole Bible where we see God give up one of his faithful followers so Satan could test him. We know it because in the end God restores Job. Maybe we even know the story of Job because of his unwavering faithfulness in the midst of horrific pain. That faithfulness is evident even at the very beginning of his story. Job says, "Naked I came from my mother's womb, and naked shall I return there; the Lord gave, and the Lord has taken away; blessed be the name of the Lord." Then the author adds the comment: "In all this Job did not sin or charge God with wrongdoing."

I don't know that I have Job's fortitude. I don't know of many who would. But his persistent faithfulness to God does give me hope that we might be stronger than we sometimes give ourselves credit for. God has created us to be resilient. And when we can't be resilient, I believe God is there to hold us up. At some point in all of our lives we will be met personally with pain and loss. We will witness violence and destruction and fear in the world around us. These things could break us. Or they could prove true that God has made us resilient and strong. With the grace and hope that only the Lord gives, we can overcome most anything. Sometimes that's really all faithfulness is – holding on to the hope that one day God will make all things good and new.

Do you believe God has created us to be strong and resilient? What things has your faith helped you overcome? Does tragedy draw you closer to God or make you push God away? Why?

Prayer:
God, you are strong. You've created me to be strong. But where I am weak you will hold me up. My faithfulness doesn't depend on the circumstances of my life or on the world around me. It depends on your love and grace that have been poured out in abundance. You are my Redeemer and my Savior. For these things I place my faith in you. Amen.

DAY 8

Scripture Reference – Psalm 27

Devotion:

Can you imagine what this world would have been like if King David and the apostle Paul had been alive at the same time? Their passion, dependence on God, and words from God are so inspiring. As Christians today, we read their words in the Old and New Testaments looking for encouragement, affirmation, promises, and hope. We share their words with friends through texts. Their words are on Pinterest, Facebook, and Twitter. Their legacy is our lifeline to God when we take the time to read them.

While reading Psalm 27, Paul's words came to my mind from Romans 8:31 when Paul says, "So what are we going to say about these things? If God is for us, who is against us?" I imagine King David would reply back with words from Psalm 27:14 saying, "Hope in the Lord! Be strong! Let your heart take courage! Hope in the Lord!"

As we journey through Lent, know that we are not alone on this journey. God's hand is upon us and watching over us just like God did for David and Paul. God's words are available to us and within us to affirm our faith and to encourage the faith of others. It is our task to be honest with God and open to the spiritual growth we need. King David and the apostle Paul grew spiritually in incredible ways. God used them each day of their lives. God can do the same in our lives.

How has God shown you that you are not alone on this journey? Do you know that God is for you? Do you hope in the Lord? Have you been honest with God, and made yourself open to the spiritual growth you need? Are there ways you yet need to be honest and open with God?

Prayer:
Holy God, give me clarity so that I may see how to grow into a deeper relationship with you. Help me to have complete trust in you like King David. Help me to share your love with others like the apostle Paul. Help me use my life to glorify you. Show me one thing today that I need to see or experience. Amen.

DAY 9

FRIDAY: TRUE CITIZENSHIP

Scripture Reference – Philippians 3:17 to 20

Devotion:

As I read through Philippians 3:17 to 20, I'm struck with what the apostle Paul has to say. He speaks of our true citizenship. We claim our temporary earthly citizenship in a particular city and country (and we, as we should, take great pride in that), but what about our eternal citizenship? Paul reminds us that beyond all things that characterize our lives, we are citizens of heaven.

This very day I had the honor and privilege to officiate the memorial service for Gloria Shaw. When meeting with Gloria's family to plan her memorial service, they shared with me an interesting story about her. Gloria's mother had lived to be ninety-eight-and-a-half years old. Gloria literally prayed to the Lord that he would not allow herself to live to be ninety-eight-and-a-half years old! It seems as though Gloria's prayer was answered, because she died at the young age of 84. But even more so than that, Gloria fought the good fight, finished the race, kept the faith, and has been awarded a crown of righteousness given to her by our righteous judge, Jesus Christ (2 Timothy 4:7 and 8).

One thing about Gloria: She knew the whereabouts of her true citizenship. Although she belonged to many clubs and organizations both in Nashville, Tennessee, and Corsicana, Texas, along with having homes in both cities as well, she was assured of her home with God in eternity. And Gloria lived as though she was bound for glory. Theodore Roosevelt once commented, "The first requisite of a good citizen in this republic of ours is that he shall be able and willing to pull his own weight." Gloria not only pulled her own weight, she served. Gloria was instrumental in getting a women's shelter off the ground in Corsicana, Texas, donated food to the food pantry, and sat on the local family services board of directors (among many other faithful activities). Gloria cared for other people. Gloria knew that "faith without works is dead" (James 2:26).

And just like Gloria, Christ "will take our weak mortal bodies and change them into glorious bodies like his own" (Philippians 3:21). Why? Because we are citizens of heaven.

Do you know where your true citizenship resides? Do you claim that citizenship? As a citizen of heaven, are you pulling your own weight?

Prayer:
Almighty God, when I get too caught up in the things of this world, and when I forget to reach out in love and support of this world's people, remind me that I am a citizen of heaven. I am bound for glory. Thank you for this promise of eternal life, made available through Jesus and his death on the cross. Thank you for this blessed true citizenship. In Jesus' name I pray. Amen.

DAY 10

SATURDAY: RESISTING GRACE

Scripture Reference – Matthew 23:37 to 39

Devotion:

Sometimes we can be so resistant to things that are actually in our best interest. For instance, I am terrible about taking care of myself when I get sick. I avoid going to the doctor, and I almost never take my medicine on time. I do that because I'm stubborn. I don't follow instructions well, even when that keeps me sick for twice as long as I should be.

I think sometimes we do the same thing with God. Even though we believe Jesus wants what's best for us, we resist following his instructions. And this is nothing new. The people of God have been resisting the Word of God forever. Jesus wasn't shy about reminding us of that. In Matthew 23:37 he cries out, "Jerusalem, Jerusalem, the city that kills the prophets and stones those who are sent to it! How often have I desired to gather your children together as a hen gathers her brood under her wings, and you were not willing!" That last little phrase, "and you were not willing," hits me hard. It reminds me of how stubborn I can be. I'm so stubborn— so set on doing things my way—that I become unwilling to listen and obey the words of my Savior. Jesus only wants to gather us close to him.

He only wants our lives to be more full of love and hope and thankfulness. When we resist his instructions, we're missing out on his grace. That's not something any of us can afford.

How can we make ourselves more open to receive the Grace of Christ? Do we really believe that God wants what's best for us? Where have you resisted the instruction of Jesus in your life?

Prayer:
God, I can be so stubborn. But you already know that. And you know the only thing that can overcome my stubbornness is your grace. Please continue to pour it out on me even when I resist letting it fill me up. Amen.

DAY 11

MONDAY: TRUSTING HIM TO DO IT

Scripture Reference – Romans 4:1 to 12

Devotion:

I love *The Message* version of this passage, especially verse 3 where it says, "Abraham entered into what God was doing for him, and *that* was the turning point. He trusted God to set him right instead of trying to be right on his own." This verse reminds me of all those times where I have been in over my head. It has happened more times than I would like to admit. Like the time I had a severe migraine driving to church to teach a class with two young children in the back seat knowing that I was going to go on call for a hospital as a chaplain at any minute. By the time I reached the church parking lot, all I could do was walk in and lie down on the office floor. It was at that point that I realized I was in over my head and I let God take over. Soon I was taken to the ER and experienced a humbling lesson… I could not do everything on my own. I needed God and others.

Abraham had a lot to brag about. He was a very successful person even before he followed God's request to pick up all that he had and follow

God. But God did not bless Abraham for his worldly success. He blessed Abraham because he turned to God and followed.

Are you at a place in life this Lent where you need to trust God to make things right instead of making them right on your own? It is a nice feeling to know that the world does not depend on you alone.

Prayer:
Help me let go of my control over the circumstance in my life. Help me to trust in your guidance and wisdom. Help me to focus more on my spiritual growth instead of my earthly gains. I trust in you, God. Thank you for your calming presence with me. Amen.

DAY 12

TUESDAY: DEALING WITH REGRET

Scripture Reference – Numbers 14:10b to 24

Devotion:

Have you ever passed up an intriguing opportunity? Have you ever skipped out on something that could have potentially been a huge win for you? Have you ever sat one out, but later wished you had rather chosen to dance? Have you ever done something you regret? I'm sure the answer to at least one of these questions is a sure and simple, "Yes."

In Numbers 14 we come face to face with one of the primary regrets of the people of Israel. They have the opportunity to enter the Promised Land (a land flowing with milk and honey) shortly after leaving Egypt and journeying through the wilderness. However, when spies are sent to check out the Promised Land, they return with bad news. They sound the alarm and incite a riot when they fearfully blurt out, "There are giants living in the Promised Land, and they will not be very happy about our presence there." The people cry, lose hope, lose faith, and forget God. God has made them an offer they can't refuse, but they refuse. They grumble. And they suffer the consequences: they are forced to wander through the barren wilderness for forty years (and only two individuals among millions get to finally enter the Promised Land). They miss the party. They miss the dance. And they regret it.

Chris Kyle believed, "It was my duty to shoot the enemy, and I don't regret it. My regrets are for the people I couldn't save: Marines, soldiers, buddies. I'm not naïve, and I don't romanticize war. The worst moments of my life have come as a SEAL. But I can stand before God with a clear conscience about doing my job." Chris Kyle didn't regret so much what he did, but rather what he didn't do, those he couldn't help, those he couldn't save. What about you? Some missed opportunities are long gone. Other opportunities are just over the horizon. Numbers 14:24 reminds us of one of the spies who had a different attitude than the others—Caleb. Caleb was ready to claim the Promised Land. Caleb was ready to trust God. Caleb didn't want to sit that one out. Caleb didn't want to die in a desert with regret. And Caleb doesn't, because he (along with Joshua) becomes one of the two Israelites who leave Egypt and forty years later get to enter the land promised to God's chosen ones. May we follow in Caleb's footsteps.

Prayer:
Almighty God, when you place opportunities in front of me, help me to do what I can. Help me to do what I must. May regret be a thing of my past, and may it be absent in my future. I want to take hold of the plans you have for my life. I want to claim the Promised Land you have in store for me, and those who will be blessed because of my faithfulness. In the holy name of Jesus I pray. Amen.

DAY 13

Scripture Reference – Luke 13:22 to 31

Devotion:

There is probably not a better way to get to know somebody than to share a meal with them. There's just something about sitting at a table while you enjoy delicious food that has the power to bring people together. Think about how most of our holiday celebrations revolve around food. At Thanksgiving, it's the turkey and dressing. For the Fourth of July, it's burgers and hot dogs. At Christmas in my family, it's my dad's baby-back ribs. Food might not always be the reason we gather, but it's certainly what we like to gather around.

Jesus also has a table that he invites us to gather around. On this side of heaven, the bread and wine of communion are served at that table, and there's always room for one more person. He doesn't turn anyone away. Jesus wants all of us there because it's at this table where the church comes together as a family to receive the grace and power it needs to be the body of Christ. But Jesus also talks about another table. This one is on the other side of heaven. He says, "Then people will come from east and west, from north and south, and will eat in the kingdom of God. Indeed, some are last who will be first, and some are first who will be last." Much like the communion table, all are invited to this table, as well. Jesus wants to know us. He wants to eat with us. He wants us to be part of the family. Unfortunately, some turn down the invitation.

I take this as a challenge, and I hope you will, too. I hope it will challenge you to build lasting and deep relationships. I hope it will encourage you to extend Jesus' invitation to the people who come into your lives so they too can feast at the heavenly banquet.

Have you accepted Christ's invitation, already? If so, how can you start extending that invitation to others? What do you hope Jesus serves at his heavenly banquet?

Prayer:
Thank you, Lord, for preparing a place at the table for me. However, I know that the more who are there, the merrier it will be. Empower me to invite those who have closed their ears to you. Let them see in me a reflection of your radical hospitality and unwavering generosity. Amen.

DAY 14

THURSDAY: THREE BECAME FOUR

Scripture Reference – Daniel 3:19 to 30

Devotion:

I have sat in a number of hospital waiting rooms. Sometimes it was in the day and sometimes it was in the deep night. No matter when I found myself there, the people around me felt like they were in the fight of their lives. Their loved one was either in surgery, sick, or even dying.

Shadrach, Meshach, and Abednego (I always love saying their names) were in the fight of their lives too. Their ruling king called for the furnace be turned up seven times hotter than normal. He wanted these men to die quickly. I imagine Shadrach, Meshach, and Abednego turned up their prayers seven times as well. Their faith was unwavering.

And then God showed up. King Nebuchadnezzar saw him first. The king saw a fourth man walking around in the furnace with the other three. All three were walking around instead of burning. In fact, when they came out of the furnace, they didn't even smell like smoke. King Nebuchadnezzar was a changed man and his kingdom changed too. Shadrach, Meshach, and Abednego were all blessed as well.

We experience fiery furnaces in our lives too. Moments when every-thing seems to be ending. Relationships, death, difficult children or par-ents, health challenges and more can create a fiery furnace season. This story from deep in the Old Testament reminds us that we are not in the furnace alone. God is right there with us. We will not be consumed. We will walk out and life will be different.

My role in the hospital waiting rooms was to remind people that God was there too. It brought comfort to the families and to me. It is easier to face a battle with God by your side than alone.

When you find yourself in a modern day fiery furnace, do you know that God is by your side? Does this great truth bring you comfort? Do you know someone going through a difficult time right now? If so, what can you do to stand with them?

Prayer:
Holy God, stand by my side today and every day. As you are with me, guide me and protect me. I pray that I have the same faith as Shadrach, Meshach, and Abednego. Help my life be a testimony to your never-ending love. Amen.

DAY 15

FRIDAY: WAKE UP!

Scripture Reference – Revelation 3:1 to 6

Devotion:

Wow! If you just read that Scripture passage from Revelation chapter 3, then you might have chills (or goose bumps). Let's recap what it says. It says some might believe that we are truly alive in Christ, but the truth is we are dead. Our faith is dead. Our walk with Jesus is dead. Our spirit is dead. It says God expects more from us (I don't know if there is anything more motivating to me than for someone to tell me that they are disappointed in me for something I did or didn't do). It says we need to repent and turn back to God, or else...

All I can say is, "Ouch!" Saint Basil once commented, "Strive to attain to the greater virtues, but do not neglect the lesser ones. Do not make light of a fall even if it be the most venial of faults; rather, be quick to repair it by repentance..." Small faults can result in enormous consequences. Seventeen percent of Americans were witnesses to this on January 28, 1986, as we watched on our television sets the launch of the Space Shuttle Challenger. What seemed like a successful launch became a disaster a mere 73 seconds later as the Challenger broke apart, killing its seven crew members and delivering a crushing blow to NASA and the world. Why did this terrible thing happen? Because of an O-ring. Small faults can result in enormous consequences.

Is there something small (or large, for that matter) that you need to repent of and give to the Lord? Maybe it's something you did to someone. Maybe it's something that should have been done, but was neglected. Maybe it's a bad attitude, prejudice, or ill will you harbor in your heart. Whatever it is, wake up, identify it, and repent. Tell God you are sorry, let go of your sin, and let him take it. Let God cleanse you of this sin. Let God make you new. Let God clothe you in white and announce to all that you are his.

Prayer:
Almighty God, it's time for me to wake up. I identify my sin of _____, and name it before you. I repent of this sin. I am sorry that I have allowed it to become a part of my life. Through the power of your Holy Spirit, I let it go. Take this sin from me, and may it never return. Father, cleanse me. Make me new. Clothe me in white. I am yours, in the precious name of Jesus. Amen.

DAY 16

SATURDAY: DEWBERRY DISCIPLES

Scripture Reference – Luke 6:43 to 45

Devotion:
My grandmother has a lot of wild dewberry bushes growing around her house. When my brother and I would go visit her when we were younger, she would hand us a bucket and tell us to go pick some dewberries for her. We would always grumble because it was hot outside and it was a hassle to get to the bushes. But we always went because we knew what fresh dewberries meant. Fresh dewberries meant homemade dewberry cobbler for dessert. That cobbler was worth every scrape and scratch we ever got. The bushes produced good fruit, and the fruit produced good dessert (with the help of my grandmother, of course).

Jesus liked to use food to describe things. He chose fruit as a way to talk about people. He said, "No good tree bears bad fruit, nor again does a bad tree bear good fruit; for each tree is known by its own fruit. Figs are not gathered from thorns, nor are grapes picked from a bramble bush" (Luke 6:43 to 44). Had my brother and I gotten to those dewberry bushes and found lemons or pinecones or even just rotten dewberries, we would've been pretty confused and pretty upset. We expect things to be what they're supposed to be and to do what they're supposed to do. That's the only way they fulfill their purpose and produce what is good and right. Our hearts are very much like those bushes. God created us to be good, and so God expects us to bear the good fruit of mercy, grace, and love with our lives. If we aren't doing that, then we are not fulfilling our purpose. The fruit that we bear will always be a good indicator of the state of our hearts. If things like anger and suspicion follow us, we should examine why that is. If things like joy, peace, patience, and kindness follow us, then our life is bearing the fruit it's supposed to bear.

What fruit are you bearing in your life? Is it good and sweet and ripe? Are your branches running dry? How might we cultivate our lives to bear more good fruit?

Prayer:
God of the land and of the rain, pour out your grace on me. Let it be like a fresh shower to a dried-out bush. Nourish me to new life so that I can produce good fruit for your kingdom. Amen.

DAY 17

MONDAY: ON JUDGING OTHERS

Scripture Reference – Romans 2:1 to 11

Devotion:
There are some things I do not understand. For instance, why did God create mosquitoes? In my mind, they are simply an annoyance for those who live in the southern states. Or why is sugar so harmful to our health when it tastes so good? Then there are bigger issues that I do not understand, like, why are there so many hungry people when our world produces enough food for everyone to eat daily? Or why do people work against each other more often than with each other?

I believe it is important to ask questions. Questions help us process the world around us. But often we are quick to move from questions to judgment. In our Scripture passage today, Paul explains how judgment, in God's eyes, is inexcusable. That is a clear and firm stance on an issue. It makes sense for God to be firm. I imagine God would prefer us to be about God's business of loving others and building up God's kingdom instead of judging others.

While thinking about this passage, I thought about reasons that I judge others. I landed on this truth about myself. I judge simply because I do not understand. And because I do not understand, I would live more like Christ if I simply tried to understand. Or even better, maybe I need to simply be at peace about all that I do not understand.

Rainer Maria Rilke wrote these words: "Be patient toward all that is unsolved in your heart and try to love the questions themselves, like locked rooms and like books that are now written in a very foreign tongue. Do not now seek the answers, which cannot be given you because you would not be able to live them. And the point is, to live everything. Live the questions now. Perhaps you will then gradually, without noticing it, live along some distant day into the answer."

Today, search your own heart and learn the reason you judge others. It will liberate you.

Prayer:
Holy God, show me my heart today. Help me let go of my judgments of others. Guide me to a life that is pleasing to you. Send me people to love and encourage. Amen.

DAY 18

Scripture Reference – Psalm 39

Devotion:

I am struck with the message that King David gives us in Psalm 39. It's best summed up in verse 4, which states, "Lord, remind me how brief my time on earth will be. Remind me that my days are numbered—how fleeting my life is."

I came across a story the other day that I'd love to share with you. It goes like this: Marvin was in the hospital on his death bed. The family called Marvin's preacher to be with him in his final moments. As the preacher stood by the bed, Marvin's condition seemed to deteriorate, and Marvin motioned for someone to quickly pass him a pen and paper. The preacher quickly got a pen and paper and lovingly handed it to Marvin. But before he had a chance to read the note, Marvin died. The preacher, feeling that now wasn't the right time to read it, put the note in his jacket pocket. It was at the funeral while speaking that the preacher suddenly remembered the note. Reaching deep into his pocket, the preacher said "and you know what, I suddenly remembered that right before Marvin died, he handed me a note. And knowing Marvin, I'm sure it was something inspiring that we can all gain from. With that introduction, the preacher ripped out the note and opened it.

The note said "**HEY, YOU ARE STANDING ON MY OXYGEN TUBE!**"

Oops! But the point is clear: life is short. Our time on earth is brief. Our days are numbered. Our lifetime is but a moment to God. Each of us is but a breath. We are travelers passing through, just as our ancestors were before us. That being the case, let's make every moment count. Let's remember that "all our busy rushing ends in nothing" (verse 6). Let's focus on the things worth focusing on: faith, family, and friends. And let's not forget that our only hope, for this world and the next, is in God.

Are you making every moment count in your life? Are you focusing on the things worth focusing on?

Prayer:
Almighty God, remind me how brief my time on earth will be. Help me to make every day, every moment, count. For you and your kingdom. In Jesus' precious name I pray. Amen.

DAY 19

WEDNESDAY: STRANGE COMPARISONS

Scripture Reference – Luke 13:18 to 21

Devotion:

Jesus talks a lot about the kingdom of God, but it seems like he never talks about it directly. He is always comparing it to something, and sometimes those comparisons seem strange and confusing. In the gospel of Luke, he does it in back-to-back parables. First, Jesus compares the kingdom of God to a tiny mustard seed that grows into a tree with birds nesting in its branches. Then, he compares it to yeast that spreads throughout a bowl of flour until it leavens the whole loaf of bread. In both of these comparisons, the kingdom of God starts small, but it soon grows and spreads until it is strong and vibrant.

When Jesus talks about the kingdom of God, he's not always talking about a far-off place in heaven. Sometimes he's talking about the kingdom he wants to establish right here and right now through us. That kingdom grows as our faith grows. What once was a small seed of faith in our hearts eventually grows and spreads and strengthens with the right nutrition and support. And eventually, our faith can grow so strong that other people can lean on us and find refuge when they need it. The kingdom of God grows as our faith in Christ grows. Some people have grown more than others, and that's okay. What's important is that we continue to let God and God's people nurture us and care for us so we can stand strong in all of life's circumstances.

How has God grown your faith throughout the years? Do others look to you for strength and support because they can see God at work in you? How can you help someone else grow and develop their faith?

Prayer:
Lord, you are my strength, and in you I place my faith. Grow me into the person you would have me to be. Fill me with your Spirit that I might bear witness to the work you are doing in my life and in this world. Amen.

DAY 20

THURSDAY: FREE

Scripture Reference – Psalm 32

Devotion:

It has been said that choosing not to forgive yourself or others is like handcuffing yourself to something that happened in the past. Because it is handcuffed to you, you are carrying it around with you everywhere you go. It is beside you when you meet new people. It is attached to you in your most joyful moments. It sleeps beside you at night. When you live with it long enough, it becomes such a close part of you that you forget it is even there. Anger and grudges are invisible, but they live with us.

Extra weight is another example. When we put on a few extra pounds and our doctor confronts us with our health, we usually work on losing the weight because we want to live longer and feel better. We might join a gym, hire a trainer, and eat less calories to lose some of weight. Weight gain is not invisible. So often we are more interested in shedding the extra pounds.

King David models for us the power of forgiveness for ourselves and others. He knows the need to be honest with God and ask for forgiveness.

He does it over and over again throughout his life. Sometimes he seeks forgiveness for big sins and sometimes he seeks forgiveness for smaller ones. In all sins he turns to God. He is honest about his mistakes and honest about his desire to do better. He understands how the lack of forgiveness can waste away a life. He also understands the freedom that comes from being forgiven.

Lent is a powerful journey. If you are in need of forgiveness for yourself or in a place where you need to forgive someone else, use this season to journey to that place. It may be time to unlock your handcuffs. It may be time to hire a trainer (friend or pastor) who will help you shed your past. It has lived with you long enough. When you come to the moment of forgiveness, you will feel free and lighter. If you are still worried about how to get there, read Psalm 32 again and be reminded that God will instruct you on how to get there.

Prayer:
Forgiving God, help me to forgive and live freely with you. Walk closely with me as I move from a life of being chained to the past to a life of being chained to you. Instruct me and teach me today and every day. Amen.

DAY 21

FRIDAY: LIVING BY FAITH

Scripture Reference – 2 Corinthians 5:6 to 15

Devotion:
One of the great truths of Christianity is what the apostle Paul reminds us of in 2 Corinthians 5:7, "For we live by faith, not by sight." There is more to reality than what we perceive with our five senses. The love of Jesus Christ "bears all things, believes all things, hopes all things, endures all things" (1 Corinthians 13:7). The love of Christ endures even death. Death is not the end, nor does it have the final say. Christ defeated death by his sacrificial death on the cross. A new world, a new reality, has opened to those who believe—an eternity called heaven.

There are so many stories of faithful men and women who lived by faith. I just today heard a story from a lady named Debbie Goodrich. Debbie is staying at my church, First United Methodist Church of Corsicana, because she is serving with an emergency response team that has come to Navarro County, Texas, to provide assistance to flood victims following the recent torrential downpours we've experienced in October 2015. One of the clients her team served was an elderly lady who 39 days ago died. The lady described to Debbie what happened. She said, "My heart stopped. I died and went to heaven. Not only did I go to heaven, but I bounced all around heaven. I saw my relatives. And you cannot begin to imagine how marvelous Jesus is!" While this "out of body" visit was taking place, the lady had been placed on life support, and when (from heaven) she heard the doctor say, "I think she's going to make it," her soul returned to her body and she breathed again. After she was finally removed from life support and was able to speak freely, she could not (and has not) stopped telling people about her special visit to heaven. And this extraordinary visit all took place because she loved someone she had never seen. She had placed her trust in a God, in a Christ, whom she had only known through faith.

How can we love someone we have never seen? This is not only possible, but very natural when we live by faith. Although life is good, the best is surely yet to be as we live by faith, not by sight.

Prayer:
Almighty God, help me to live by faith and not by sight. Don't let me be fooled into thinking or feeling that what I perceive with my five senses is all there is. There indeed is a spiritual realm of which you are a part, and I am a part. Give me courage and strength to live for Christ who died and was raised again. In the name of the risen Christ I pray. Amen.

DAY 22

SATURDAY: JOY IN HEAVEN

Scripture Reference – Luke 15:1 to 10

Devotion:
I think maybe one of the most important questions we can ask ourselves as Christians is: What makes our God happy? What brings Christ joy? We could probably answer that in a lot of ways. We make God happy by caring for people who are sick and hungry. The Lord finds joy when we give ourselves sacrificially or when our lives are full of peace, mercy, and love. I believe that is all true. God is happy with us when we do the things God asks us to do. We should keep doing them. But the gospel of Luke says there is something else that makes God happy which we cannot overlook. Jesus says in Luke, "There will be more joy in heaven over one sinner who repents than over ninety-nine righteous persons who need no repentance" (Luke 15:7).

The Lord our God, along with all of heaven, is filled with joy when a sinner repents. I grew up thinking this verse was about that one major moment of repentance where we turn away from our life of sin and accept Jesus as our Savior. And, certainly, God is happy in that moment. Repentance, though, is not a one-time act. Even after Christ welcomes us into his loving arms, there are still times in our lives when we must ask for forgiveness and seek reconciliation. As Christians, we know that we are constantly turning away from God, even when we don't mean to or want to. That's why God gave us the gift of repentance. Every time we fall to our knees and turn away from our mistakes, we will find the warm embrace of our Savior. Every time we repent, heaven celebrates because we were lost, and then we were found.

How long has it been since you repented before God? Why is it important that we continue to repent and seek forgiveness throughout our entire walk of faith? Why is repentance sometimes so hard for us to do?

Prayer:
God, you are so big. You refuse to be driven away by my sin and my mistakes. Thank you for never leaving me or forsaking me. Thank you for keeping your arms held wide for me every time I turn back to you. I repent of the things that separate me from you and from the things that separate me from those that I love. Find joy in this act of humility. Find joy in offering me your forgiveness. Amen.

DAY 23

MONDAY: BREAK A RULE

Scripture Reference – Leviticus 23:26 to 41

Devotion:

This passage from Leviticus causes me to feel stressed. It reminds me of being in elementary school. There were so many rules to follow. So many opportunities to make mistakes. So much to process in addition to learning the lessons for the day. In third grade Mrs. Hagelstein was my teacher. The two of us did not get along as far as I can remember. I am sure she was a fine educator, but my third grade brain felt stress often in her classroom. One day she saw me talking with a friend in my class. She immediately asked my friend and me to join her at the front of the room and continue our conversation in front of the class. Of course I was humiliated. One reason I was humiliated is because my friend was a boy who went to church with me. The other reason was because I had been caught breaking one of her rules. She had a lot of rules.

Moses and God had a lot of rules too that were needed to guide God's people on their journey. Leviticus is full of these rules. It is fascinating to read through them and imagine living life with them. The rules were ways for God's people to experience peace and experience God. They were necessary and good.

But I can't help but be thankful for Jesus. Through the death of Jesus, we experienced atonement. Jesus took our place on the cross. He took our sins on as his own. He gave us life with a few simple rules, love God and love others, instead of a lot of rules. This is the most precious gift we have ever received. Let's be thankful.

In our thankfulness, let's remember to refrain from making up rules that cause people around us to feel stressed. Dinner doesn't always have to be served at the same time if someone is running late. Isn't it more important to be together? Children can stay up a little later to finish a movie with the family instead of upsetting the whole evening demanding that the TV be turned off. Our homes do not need to be perfectly clean to have company over. And it's OK if your family just needs to skip a practice, game, or some appointment. Some days breaking a rule might just help you feel more alive and less beat down.

If you do decide to break a rule and run into another Mrs. Hagelstein in this world, just smile and share with her your love of Jesus. Talk about how much you love God and others in front of all the people around you. Maybe that is what I should have done back in third grade.

Prayer:
Loving God, on this day help me to see rules in my life that are unnecessary. Help me to clean them out of my life so that I may live more simply. Thank you for Jesus and his gift to me on the cross. I am thankful to be forgiven. Send me someone today that I may love because you love me. Amen.

DAY 24

TUESDAY: WHO WILL COME TO OUR RESCUE?

Scripture Reference – Psalm 53

Devotion:
Psalm 53 paints a pretty ugly picture of humankind. Verses (directed towards humanity) such as, "… not one of them does good!" (verse 1), and "… all have turned away; all have become corrupt. No one does good, not a single one!" (verse 3) cause us to squirm. We don't like, nor do we want, to hear that kind of message. However, the Bible is full of this message. God's Word reminds us time and time again of humankind's predisposition to sin. Paul reminds us in Romans 3:23 that, "all have sinned and fall short of the glory of God." It's been said, "Only two ingredients are needed for sin: desire and opportunity!" We don't want to hear it, but this message is the truth of our human condition.

But (praise God!) that isn't the end of our story. The psalmist brings to our attention that long ago God had a plan to restore his people. The question is asked, "Who will come from Mount Zion to rescue Israel?" (verse 6). The answer is simple: Jesus will come to rescue Israel. And Jesus not only came to rescue Israel, but all of us who will choose to turn from our sin towards the Lord. On September 11th, 2001, the world became aware of the heroic first responders who willingly ran up the stairs to rescue those trapped in the Twin Towers. And our God heroically came down to earth from heaven to rescue you and me—from our sin.

The question is, will you say, "Yes" to your rescuer? Will you go with the One who came from heaven to earth, and allow God to lead you down his path of righteousness (Psalm 23:3) that ends in abundant living here on earth and eternal life in heaven? I pray you will. And I pray you will again. And again. And again.

Prayer:
Almighty God, thank you for the amazing grace you give to me. You came to rescue me from my sin. You came to restore me to yourself. Because of your love, I will shout with joy. Because of your mercy, I will rejoice eternally. I say, "Yes" to you. Lead me down your path of righteousness all of my days, and I will dwell in your house forever.

Day 25

Scripture Reference – 2 Kings 4:1 to 7

Devotion:

Sometimes when I'm reading Biblical stories—especially Old Testament stories I haven't read in a while—the smallest little details start to stick out to me. That happened as I read about the prophet Elisha and how he performs the miracle with the widow's oil. She keeps pouring and pouring and pouring, but her jar never runs empty. We can see that jar of oil as an image of God's mercy and grace. Our Lord pours them out on us in abundance, and they will never run dry. That is very good news because we desperately need God's abundant mercy and grace in our lives. However, the detail that caught my eye wasn't the abundant oil, it was the empty vessels that the widow poured the oil into. Elisha tells her, "'Go outside, borrow vessels from all your neighbors, empty vessels and not just a few...' So she left him and shut the door behind her and her children; they kept bringing vessels to her, and she kept pouring" (2 Kings 4:3 and 5).

While God was busy providing an abundance of oil, this widow's neighbors were busy providing her with an abundance of empty vessels for the oil. Because of their generosity, these neighbors helped make God's miracle as powerful and life-changing as it possibly could be. What a bless-ing they were to this widow by allowing themselves to be used in such a simple way by God! Our Lord transformed their empty vessels into vessels of life and hope. God wants to do the same thing through us. The Lord of abundance simply asks us to give what we have to heaven's purposes. When we do that, God's miracles can reach their fullest and most grace-filled potential.

What are you giving to the service of God? Do you hold anything back? How have your brothers and sisters in Christ helped make a gift from God even better?

Prayer:
Lord, not only do you give in abundance, but you give me neighbors and friends who will give in abundance, too. Thank you for their faithfulness to you, and their willingness to serve others wherever and however they can. Help me find the willingness to do the same. Amen.

DAY 26

THURSDAY: BLESS ME

Scripture Reference – Psalm 126

Devotion:
Do you remember the last time God did something great in your life? Where were you? What were you doing before God showed up? A few weeks ago, this happened to me. It was on a Saturday. We were having a normal day. We had a few things on our calendar but not too many. And then our friends knocked on our door. They came into our home. They brought gifts for our children. We visited around our kitchen table all day. Laughter and joy were everywhere. We made dinner reservations and enjoyed dinner together at one of our favorite local restaurants. The food was delicious. The time together was life-giving. It was wonderful. God was all around us that day. We too were overjoyed like the author of the psalm reading.

The promising part of the psalm that I love is that God can do it all again. God can take our current circumstances and bring laughter into them. God can take our mundane schedule and shower us with joy. God can turn our distress into blessings. We simply must ask.

Socrates said, "Our prayers should be for blessings in general, for God knows best what is good for us." On this day, let's trust God and ask God to bless us. Who knows who might knock on our door, call us on the phone, text us a message, or simply give us a smile at the store. God has blessed us before and God will do it again. That is just how God works.

Prayer:
Bless me, God. You have filled my life with joy and laughter before and I know you will do it again. I thank you for all the many ways you have shown your love for me. Bless me so that I can continue to be a blessing to others in your name. Amen.

DAY 27

FRIDAY: THERE IS NO OTHER GOD

Scripture Reference – Isaiah 43:8 to 15

Devotion:

Perhaps you've heard the joke about the time when Jesus, Moses, and an old bearded guy are all playing golf together. They get to the first hole and it's a long one with a big deep water hazard in the middle. Jesus takes a shot. It lands on this tiny patch of dirt on the right edge of the hazard. Jesus doesn't want to take a penalty for a drop and he stinks at shooting left handed, so he decides to just walk out on the water and make his shot. It lands on the green and he puts it in. Birdie. Moses steps up. He takes a shot. This one is going right into the center of the hazard. Moses raises his hands and parts the waters. The ball lands. Moses walks out and takes his shot. It lands on the green and he puts it in. Birdie. The old bearded guy steps up to the tee. He takes his shot. It too is going straight into the water hazard. It heads straight for a lily pad with a frog on it. The frog sees the ball and thinks that it is a fly. It shoots out its tongue and swallows the ball. Right at that moment a hawk flies over and snatches the frog in its talons and flies away. As it flies over the green the hawk squeezes tightly and the frog gasps dropping the ball out of its mouth. The ball falls from the sky straight into the hole. Hole in one. Moses turns to Jesus and says, "I hate playing with your dad."

Yes, it is true that God has done (and will continue to do) some amazing things. Creation of the universe, miracles, and divine initiatives are all a part of God's portfolio. There is no other god worth worshipping. There is no other god before whom we bow. In fact, there is no other god… period. Chris Tomlin's worship song, "Our God," reminds us, "Our God is greater. Our God is stronger. God, you are higher than any other. Our God is healer. Awesome in power. Our God! Our God!" Isaiah prophesies, "… I alone am God. There is no other God—there never has been, and there never will be. I, yes I, am the Lord, and there is no other Savior" (Isa. 43:10 and 11). And the apostle Peter testifies to the Jewish Council in Acts 4, "There is salvation in no one else! God has given no other name under heaven by which we must be saved" (verse 12).

John Wesley once commented, "Bring me a worm that can comprehend a man, and then I will show you a man that can comprehend the Triune God." God is indeed so great. Yet this great God put on flesh and came near to us in Jesus so that we might know his true nature of unconditional love, and his deep desire for us to live eternally in relationship with him. There truly is salvation in no one (or nothing) else. There is no other God. There never has been, and there never will be.

To whom do you look for salvation? To yourself? To money, or other material possessions? Have you experienced the greatness of our God? Do you have a personal relationship with God through Jesus Christ? Are you enjoying that relationship? And if so, how?

Prayer:
Almighty God, thank you for your greatness. Thank you for your nearness. There is salvation in no one and nothing else. There is no other God, but you. There never has been, and there never will be. Thank you, Jesus, for this wonderful truth! In your great name I pray. Amen.

DAY 28

SATURDAY: WHERE IS JESUS?

Scripture Reference – John 11:45 to 57

Devotion:
Jesus wants to be at the center of our lives. He wants to fill us up with hope and grace and love each and every day. But sometimes I think we push him to the fringes. Maybe we are afraid to let him in close because of how his presence challenges us to be better. Maybe we fear what he will ask us to do. Whatever the reasons, sometimes we would just prefer Jesus to stay out in the wilderness.

Even while Jesus walked on the earth, people tried to push him out of view. The Pharisees were the primary culprits. In fact, they decided killing Jesus was the only way to keep him from disrupting their lives. After Jesus learns this news in the gospel of John, this is what the author writes: "Jesus therefore no longer walked about openly among the Jews, but went from there to a town called Ephraim in the region near the wilderness; and he remained there with the disciples" (John 11:54). This verse makes me sad. So far in John, Jesus' ministry has been one of healing. He is bringing help and hope to the Jewish people. But their leaders fear his power. So they push him away. They force him outside of the city and into the wilderness.

Jesus lives on the fringes of the city for some time, and he will live on the fringes of our lives if we push him there.

Is Jesus at the center of your life in everything you do, or are there some situations where you force him into the wilderness? How would your life change if Jesus was always at the center? Are you sometimes afraid to let Christ close? Why?

Prayer:
Remind me, God of mercy and grace, that you only desire what is best for me. You love me, yet I push you away. I fear what my life might become if I place you at the center of everything I am and do. Relieve that fear. Make of me whatever you wish. Amen.

DAY 29

Scripture Reference – Hebrews 10:19 to 25

Devotion:

The other day in a fast-food kid's meal, my daughter was given a VIP badge and necklace. She wore it during lunch and the rest of the day. She loved it (for a day). The next day when the new toy began to lose its new-toy appeal, she read the letters, VIP, and asked me what it meant. I shared with her that it means "very important person." She seemed to believe that her necklace was the right necklace for her.

A VIP (very important person) is a person who is accorded special privileges due to his or her status or importance. Maybe you have been given VIP status at a concert or another event. This status opens doors that are shut to the general public. It blesses the person with "extras" in life and increases their level of comfort.

We too are important for two reasons. The first is that we are loved so much by God that God's Son took away our sin and gave us a fresh start in return. We are also important because we have very important work to do while we walk around on Earth. We have the task of "sparking love and good deeds" around us each and every day.

When you read this passage in Hebrews, I hope you will feel like a VIP. According to Hebrews (and other Scriptures), Christ makes all who believe in him very important people. We become people with spiritual "extras" and our joy of life increases. Christ did this for us on the cross. In that one amazing act of love and sacrifice, our status changed from average to important. And the Christian VIP status is available to everyone instead of only a select few.

I hope you stop by a fast-food restaurant soon and receive a VIP pass. It will remind you how important you really are to Christ. But maybe we already wear that badge around our necks through the cross necklaces that so many of us wear daily. When you worship together this week, remember that you are all very important people with a very important mission. Love God and love others.

Prayer:
Dear Jesus, thank you for your gift to me. I am thankful I am loved and important in your eyes. I pray for more times to sit with you in stillness to feel your love. I also pray for opportunities to do good deeds in your name. Amen.

DAY 30

TUESDAY: STOP STRUGGLING!

Scripture Reference – Judges 9:7 to 15

Devotion:
One of the great themes of history (including the period of the judges and the kings of Israel) is the great struggle for power. Kingdoms are built. Kingdoms topple. Kings ascend to the throne. Other kings replace them. There is a place I love to go when I visit my parents in northwest Louisiana. It's called the Bayou Pierre Alligator Farm. One of the attractions of this alligator farm is a lagoon where there are dozens of gators, and periodically throughout the day they are fed. When feeding time comes, a couple of people row a barge into the middle of the lagoon, attach raw chicken parts to metal rods, and then hang the pieces over the side of the barge until an alligator lunges out of the water and SNAP! What's interesting to me is that the largest alligator around the barge seems to be the one who always gets the raw chicken. But what seems to be the case (with alligators and life in general) is that there is always a bigger alligator.

So it becomes very important for followers of Jesus Christ to recognize that this struggle for power (and maintaining an "I, me, mine" attitude) in our world is petty, misguided, and quite the opposite of what Jesus has in mind for his disciples. The truth is, we have a King who is all powerful, and his name is Jesus. But this King of kings did not struggle for power one bit. In fact, our King gave up his throne in heaven to come to us. Our King rejected power that was offered to him by Satan. Our King did not wear a crown of gold and precious jewels, but rather a crown of thorns that brought him great pain and made him bleed. Our King was arrested, mocked, beaten, crucified, yet three days later he rose from the dead. Our King was, "… pierced for our transgressions, he was crushed for our iniquities; the punishment that brought us peace was upon him, and by his wounds we are healed" (Isaiah 53:5). Our King came to this earth not to be served, but to serve.

And our King has invited us to join him in his kingdom. Jesus has called us to come and die, as is recorded in Luke 9:23, "All who want to come after me must deny themselves, take up their cross daily, and follow me." So let's stop struggling for power, and follow the way of our King.

Do you find yourself struggling for power? How can you follow in Jesus' footsteps?

Prayer:
Almighty God, in my human condition I crave more and more power. But this is not the way of Jesus. The way of Christ is the way of love, service, and sacrifice. Help me to follow his way, rather than my way. Help me to stop trying to build my kingdom, and focus all my efforts on building your kingdom. In Jesus' name I pray. Amen.

DAY 31

WEDNESDAY: POLYNOMIAL PROBLEMS

Scripture Reference – Luke 18:31 to 34

Devotion:

One of my least favorite things in the world is when I can't understand something. That feeling of frustration gets me so upset and makes me feel so embarrassed. In my mind, if other people can figure it out, then I should be able to figure it out. I remember this one time during my senior year of high school when I just could not wrap my mind around polynomials in my precalculus math class. Math was never my greatest subject, but usually I could get by okay. There was no getting by polynomials. No amount of teaching or example problems could help me understand what a polynomial was and why on earth it was so important for me to figure out.

Not being able to understand something is never any fun. That's why I feel so much sympathy for the disciples. Sometimes they just can't wrap their minds around what Jesus is trying to teach them. Maybe the best example is when Jesus sits them down in the gospel of Luke to tell them what is about to happen—that he will soon suffer and die but then be resurrected. Luke writes of the disciples after that conversation, "But they understood nothing about all these things; in fact, what he said was hidden from them, and they did not grasp what was said" (Luke 18:34). They just can't understand what's happening. The disciples can't wrap their minds around the thought of a world where Jesus wasn't there in the flesh with them. I can't even imagine their frustration, and I'm glad I don't ever have to be put in their shoes. We have the gift of hindsight. And we know how the story ultimately ends. It ends with our Savior dying, rising, and one day coming again to make the world new. Praise God we can concern ourselves with things like polynomials because we never have to feel confused by Christ's plans for redemption.

Even though we know how our story ends, what are some of the things in our faith that are hard for you to wrap your mind around? Can you remember feeling frustrated or embarrassed because you couldn't figure something out? What was that experience like?

Prayer:
Jesus, Lord and Savior, thank you for giving me the confidence of your grace and love. Give me understanding in the things I question and doubt. Give me the faith and the patience to be okay with not knowing all the answers. You are enough. Amen.

DAY 32

THURSDAY: SUFFERING WITH PURPOSE

Scripture Reference – Isaiah 53:10 to 12

Devotion:

Mother Theresa (d. 1997) understood the role of suffering for God's people. She committed her life to simplicity and loving those who were left with no one to love them because of their illness. William Tyndale (d. 1536) understood the role of suffering for God's mission. He translated the New Testament into everyday English instead of Latin, challenged the Catholic Church about their control over the sacred Word, and was executed before he could finish the Old Testament. God understands suffering for the forgiveness of all and fully knew what he was asking of his Son Jesus Christ when he sent him to live among us and die for us.

Suffering is a powerful theme throughout the Bible. Romans 5:4 to 5 says, "We even take pride in our problems, because we know that trouble produces endurance, endurance produces character, and character produces hope. This hope doesn't put us to shame, because the love of God has been poured out in our hearts through the Holy Spirit, who has been given to us." When our "normal" life is suddenly interrupted with a "crisis," we can find rest in the fact that God is there too and fully understands the suffering that will follow the crisis. God also fully understands the value to moving through a difficult season. We will be changed and the world around us will be changed. If we live through such a season with God in mind, people around us will also be changed and move closer to God.

This is exactly what Jesus did for us. This is exactly what we remember during this season of Lent. Jesus fulfilled his mission. He carried his cross to the end. He endured the pain of death and humiliation. He did not take the power within his reach to stop events from happening. He lived through them with his eyes focused on God. Because he did this, the world changed and all who know him even today are changed.

When we journey through a difficult moment, day, week, or season, we know that we are not alone. God is there with us. We also know that our suffering will leave us changed and we will grow closer to God. Just as God placed Jesus beside him as our intercessor in eternal life, God will welcome us to eternal life when our earthly life comes to an end. We understand the role of suffering because through Jesus' suffering we are saved.

Prayer:
Thank you, Jesus, for saving me. Thank you for being my companion during difficult days. Thank you for understanding the ways that I suffer. I pray that my life will reflect your love and hope to people who I meet. I pray that in my suffering your message will shine bright. Amen.

DAY 33

FRIDAY: IN GOOD HANDS

Scripture Reference – Psalm 31:9 to 16

Devotion:
Remember the story about the fellow who was stuck on his rooftop in a flood. He was praying to God for help. Soon a man in a canoe came by and the fellow shouted to the man on the roof, "Jump in, I can save you." The stranded fellow shouted back, "No, it's OK, I'm praying to God and he is going to save me." So the canoe went on. Then a motorboat came by. The fellow in the motorboat shouted, "Jump in, I can save you." To this the stranded man said, "No thanks, I'm praying to God and he is going to save me. I have faith." So the motorboat went on. Then a helicopter came by and the pilot shouted down, "Grab this ladder and I will lift you to safety." To this the stranded man again replied, "No thanks, I'm praying to God and he is going to save me. I have faith." So the helicopter reluctantly flew away. Soon the water rose above the rooftop and the man drowned. He went to Heaven. He finally got his chance to discuss this whole situation with God, at which point he exclaimed, "I had faith in you but you didn't save me, you let me drown. I don't understand why!" To this God replied, "I sent you a canoe and a motorboat and a helicopter, what more did you expect?"

It's one thing (and a very important thing) to cry out to God in times of trouble and distress. That being said, it's quite another thing to look around and be aware of the many ways God is answering those prayers, responding to our cries for help, and bestowing his divine mercy upon us. Like King David, might we say, "But I am trusting you, O Lord, saying, 'You are my God!' My future is in your hands... Let your favor shine on your servant. In your unfailing love, rescue me... How great is the goodness you have stored up for those who fear you. You lavish it on those who come to you for protection, blessing them before the watching world... Praise the Lord, for he has shown me the wonders of his unfailing love... So be strong and courageous, all you who put your hope in the Lord!" (Psalm 31:14, 16, 19, 21, and 24). Because of God's great love for us, we are in good hands!

Do you cry out to God in times of trouble and distress? Are you aware of the ways God is answering your cries? Can you, like King David, say, "But I am trusting you, O Lord?"

Prayer:
Almighty God, thank you for keeping me safe in the past, for holding me in the present, and for promising me a future. I praise you for the mercy and protection you give me. My hope is in you. In Jesus' name I pray. Amen.

DAY 34

SATURDAY: A STRANGER AND A FRIEND

Scripture Reference – Luke 22:1 to 13

Devotion:

I'm the kind of person that enjoys talking to strangers. If I'm standing in line at the grocery store or waiting for a flight at the airport, more than likely I'm going to strike up a conversation with the person next to me. Sometimes they are receptive and talk back; sometimes they don't. I remember during one flight, I talked to the guy next to me on the plane about music and guitars for two hours. I don't know why, but sometimes it's just easy to open up to a stranger.

The Bible talks a lot about how we are supposed to welcome the stranger. Jesus definitely did that. But during the Last Supper, Jesus was on the opposite end of the welcome. He was welcomed as a stranger. When he is giving Peter instructions for the preparation of the Passover meal, this is what Jesus says: "When you have entered the city, a man carrying a jar of water will meet you; follow him into the house he enters and say to the owner of the house, 'The teacher asks you, "Where is the guest room, where I may eat the Passover with my disciples?"'" He will show you a large room upstairs, already furnished" (Luke 22:10 to 12a). This random man with the water jar welcomes Jesus and all of the disciples into his house for the Passover meal. Jesus and the disciples are strangers to him, yet he prepares them a room. Maybe he had heard of Jesus or maybe he hadn't. Either way, this man with the water jar isn't satisfied with being a stranger to Jesus. He wants to welcome Jesus as a friend. Christ has given us the same opportunity to call him "friend." We were once strangers to our God, but Christ redeemed us and called us his own. Thanks be to God.

How can you offer the hospitality that Christ and this man offered to people in your life? Are we still called to welcome the stranger? What are some things we can do to make the strangers among us feel more welcome and at home?

Prayer:
Lord, you came as a stranger into this world. Throughout your life, you traveled through cities and towns as a wondering migrant. Sometimes you were welcomed, and sometimes you were not. I want to welcome you into my life. I want to be more gracious and more hospitable. I want you to stay with me as a friend and as a teacher. Make me more like you. Amen.

DAY 35

MONDAY: ADJUST THE LENS

Scripture Reference – Isaiah 42: 1 to 9

Devotion:
God is always at work even when we do not notice. Always. Often our lives create a rhythm that moves us from one day to the next or one season to the next without much change in our spiritual lives or lives in general. But when something different happens and our rhythm is forced to change, we notice. First we notice the immediate changes around us, then the "why" questions begin to form. We want to know why our life is being affected. How quickly can we get back to our old rhythm? How long will this new rhythm last? If we were looking through a camera lens, the lens would be focused on our life only. It would not show what is happening beyond what we can see. It would not show us what God is doing.

God's people in Isaiah were experiencing a close-up-lens moment. They were confused about the reasons God did not protect them from the Babylonians who destroyed their temple and centuries of possessions. God had always protected them. Why were they defeated this time? This passage from Isaiah invites God's people to see the whole picture, not just their part. God wanted them to see how God planned to send a servant to bring justice to all people. God also wanted the people to understand that they have an active part in the fulfillment of God's plan. They did not have the option to sit on the sidelines and watch. God needed them and God needs us to carry out God's work for God's kingdom.

What is your lens focused on today in your life? Are you aware of the way God is working around you to fulfill his purpose for you? Are you aware of the way you can help God build the kingdom on Earth? Every day is a good day to adjust our lens and our perspective on life. Spending too much time only focused on ourselves may cause us to miss out on all that God has to show us. God is always at work when we do not notice. Always.

Prayer:
Help me, God, to be aware of my role in your work. Use my hands and my feet to love those around me so that your kingdom may grow starting with me. Thank you for creating me in such a way that I can know you without always seeing you. I find comfort knowing you are at work in my life and the lives of others. I pray my life rhythm stays in sync with your rhythm. Amen.

DAY 36

TUESDAY: LIVE TO TELL

Scripture Reference – John 12:20 to 36

Devotion:

If someone came up to you and asked, "Sir (or Ma'am), I want to meet Jesus," what would you say? What would you tell them? How would you reveal the risen Christ to them? It's interesting, but people have all kinds of ideas and opinions about Jesus and his followers. Some of the provocative images that outsiders have of Christianity include: A pack of domesticated cats that look like they are thinking deep thoughts, but are really just waiting for their next meal. An ostrich with its head in the sand. A hobby that diverts people's attention. A powerful amplifier being undermined by poor wiring and weak speakers.

Wow, those are not images for which the Church should be proud! Robert Lewis Stevenson once entered in his diary, as if recording an extraordinary phenomenon, "I have been to Church today, and am not depressed." American humorist Oliver Wendell Holmes once wrote, "I might have entered the ministry if certain clergy I knew had not looked and acted so much like undertakers." So back to my question: how would you describe the Son of God to someone wanting to experience him? I think Jesus tells us in this Scripture from John 12 not so much what to say, but what to do. We don't tell them about Jesus, we show them Jesus. We give our life away. We die to self—and in doing so we reap a harvest of new lives for Christ and for God's glory. This is what Jesus did. As John reminds us in verse 32, when Jesus was lifted up on the cross, he drew everyone to himself. He shared his life. He gave his life. And through this act of self-denial, we come to know him. We come to know God.

So what do we do? We live to tell. May our lives loudly proclaim the Gospel of Jesus Christ. Or as Saint Francis put it, "Preach the Gospel at all times and when necessary use words."

Prayer:
Almighty God, help me to preach the Gospel at all times and when necessary use words. I truly desire to reveal the risen Christ to a world in darkness. Help me to remember that it's not through fancy words and clever persuasion that I do this, but rather through a life faithfully lived. In Jesus' holy name I pray. Amen.

DAY 37

WEDNESDAY: BETTER TOGETHER

Scripture Reference – Hebrews 12:1 to 3

Devotion:
I love team sports. My favorite is basketball. I grew up playing basketball. When I played in high school, I spent hours and hours in the gym alone, shooting the ball, working on my ball handling, and trying to get in shape so I could be the best player I was capable of being. However, I knew that none of that mattered if I didn't learn how to be a good teammate. Basketball isn't an individual sport. I was better because I was on a team. My teammates could push me to get better in practice, and we could all perform better in the games when we worked together.

Christianity is a lot like that. It is sort of like a team sport, and we are better when we are in community with one another. The writer of Hebrews would agree, I think. He says, "Therefore, since we are surrounded by so great a cloud of witnesses, let us also lay aside every weight and the sin that clings so closely, and let us run with perseverance the race that is set before us, looking to Jesus the pioneer and perfecter of our faith" (Hebrews 12:1-2a). Christianity is not meant to be done solo. We need each other, and Jesus knows that. That's why he gave us the church. The people who make up the church are our great cloud of witnesses. They give us support when we are weak. They cheer us on when we grow tired. They run along-side us as we make our way towards Jesus, together. I know I'm glad God doesn't expect me to do the work of the kingdom all by myself. I hope you are, too. I pray you have a community that will journey through this life of faith with you.

Are you part of a thriving Christian community? What do you think your roles are on your team of faith? How has your church helped you persevere through hard times in your life? How has it challenged you to grow as a disciple?

Prayer:
Lord, thank you for not expecting me to live my life alone. You created humanity for community, and you gave me that community through my brothers and sisters in Christ. Help me to be the best teammate I can pos-sibly be. Teach the church how to work together so we can run our race towards you with grace and humility. Amen.

DAY 38

MAUNDY THURSDAY: READY TO GO

Scripture Reference – Exodus12:1 to 14

Devotion:
In the car on the way to summer camp with my daughter when she was 9, we asked her how she was feeling. She said she was "nercited." There was not a word to describe her feeling, so she created a new one. She was both nervous and excited. Months before camp, we received a packing list of all the items she needed to bring to camp. It was very detailed. As the weeks went by we packed each item into her trunk. Her luggage was ready. Her care packages were carefully labeled. The day had come and we were driving her closer and closer to a new experience. If I'm honest, we were all a little "nercited."

I imagine the word "nercited" could be applied to the Israelites as well on the night of the first Passover. Their time had come. They were experiencing a change in power and life. They were on the edge of being liberated from slavery. I would hope they were excited about the life that was before them. I hope they were ready to pack up and leave. But my human side tells me that they were probably nervous and excited. God gave them detailed instructions on their first Passover meal. Each item on their menu, like flat bread, was meant to prepare them for their quick departure. The bitter herbs reminded them of their suffering. Cooking over the fire instead of water reminded them of the burning bush. God told them to eat with their sandals on and their walking stick in hand. Change was coming and they needed to be ready.

Often God invites us to move on as well from bondage to freedom. Maybe you are in a job that is causing you more harm than good. Maybe you are in a relationship that needs to end. Maybe it is time to go to school or back to school. Maybe it is time to heal a relationship that is keeping you from moving forward. In all of these situations I can imagine that you may feel "nercited" about a change, but God is working to do something amazing in your life. Do you really want to stop God's plan? Instead, consider marking the door to your life with a sign of God. Pray. Talk with a friend. Attend worship. Let God in and step outside your comfort zone. It's time to move on to the next chapter of life.

If you are "nercited," that is just fine. You are working with God and God is leading you on your own path so that you can join others on a well-paved path to the promise land.

Prayer:
Holy God, calm my fears. Comfort me with Scripture as I make changes in my life. Guide my steps. Help me to see where change is needed. Help me to know you are with me. Give me the courage that I need to take the first step. Amen.

DAY 39

GOOD FRIDAY: ABANDONED AND FORSAKEN

Scripture Reference – Psalm 22

Devotion:

Today we observe Good Friday. This is the day we remember Jesus' ultimate sacrifice: his betrayal, his arrest, his corrupt interrogation by the Jewish authorities, his unlawful imprisonment, the false accusations directed towards him before Pontius Pilate, his humiliation, the torture, the beating, how the crowd chose to have a violent rascal named Barabbas released instead of Jesus, his crucifixion, and his death. William H. Willimon states, "Despite our earnest efforts, we couldn't climb all the way up to God. So what did God do? In an amazing act of condescension, on Good Friday, God climbed down to us, became one with us. The story of divine condescension begins on Christmas and ends on Good Friday."

On Good Friday we remember how Jesus was completely rejected by friend and foe. It's no wonder why, from the cross, Jesus recited Psalm 22:1, "My God, my God, why have you forsaken me?" (Matthew 27:46). Jesus truly was abandoned and forsaken. But Jesus was not completely abandoned and forsaken. There was one who would not let go of him, and Jesus knew this very well. That One is God, Jesus' own Father. Jesus recites Psalm 22:1 from the cross not so much because he felt forsaken and abandoned, but rather as a reminder of how that Psalm ends. Verse 24 of Psalm 22 reminds us why we must praise the Lord, "For he has not ignored or belittled the suffering of the needy. He has not turned his back on them, but has listened to their cries for help." As Jesus died an agonizing death on the cross, he was not assured of God's absence. Rather, and quite the opposite, Jesus was assured of God's presence. Jesus trusted and relied on his Father on this darkest of days, during this most horrific hour. And in doing so, he showed us the way. Even when we walk through the valley of the shadow of death, we will fear no evil, for our Shepherd is with us (Psalm 23:4). We never walk alone. We are never abandoned and forsaken.

Do you know that you never walk alone? In good times and bad, do you know that God is listening to you? Do you know that God is holding you? Do you rely on the Lord during difficult seasons?

Prayer:
Almighty God, thank you for Good Friday. On Good Friday you defeated sin. On Good Friday you defeated death. I have victory because of your gracious activity on Good Friday. I cannot truly express the gratitude I have for Christ's sacrifice on the cross. But even so, I must say, "Thank you. Thank you, Jesus." It is in your redeeming name I pray. Amen.

DAY 40

HOLY SATURDAY: RISEN, INDEED!

Scripture Reference – Matthew 27:57 to 66

Devotion:

Pilate and the Pharisees go to extreme measures to make sure Jesus stays in his tomb. There is already a large stone covering the entrance, but that's not enough for them. In the gospel of Matthew they actually seal the stone shut and send Roman soldiers to guard it against intruders. They worry the disciples will steal the body, so they plan to stay for three whole days just to make certain Jesus doesn't go anywhere. The Pharisees say to Pilate, "Sir, we remember what that impostor said while he was still alive, 'After three days I will rise again.' Therefore command the tomb to be made secure until the third day; otherwise his disciples may go and steal him away" (Matthew 27:63 to 64b). These Pharisees aren't just satisfied with Jesus being dead. They want the whole movement he started to die, too.

On this final day of Lent, I say "Praise God that they failed!" Not only did they fail to keep Jesus in the tomb, they failed to stop his message of love and grace from erupting out of it and spreading throughout the whole world. With Lent coming to a close, this is the good news we are getting ready to proclaim. On Easter morning, the church will shout, "He is risen!

Risen, indeed!" A stone and some guards could not hold our Savior. Death could not hold our Savior. The tomb is empty, our Savior lives, and his message is still being spread to the ends of the earth. The journey of Lent has been a journey towards this moment when we remember the power of resurrection and the hope that comes with it. As Christians, we are Easter people. We are filled by the life and the love and the strength of our God who lives and reigns forever and ever. Shout that message loud!

What have you learned over the course of your Lenten journey this year? Do you feel like Lent has prepared you for the glorious celebration of Easter morning? How do you hope hearing the good news of Easter this year will affect how you live every day going forward?

Prayer:
Conqueror of death and giver of life, you are great and you are strong. You died so that I could live. You arose so that I might have eternal life. The grace and mercy that erupted out of your tomb on Easter morning are still filling up this world. They are still filling me up. But may they not just fill me. May they change me. May they grow me. May they sanctify me until my time comes to meet you face to face. Amen.

CONCLUSION

Perhaps you've heard the story about the passenger who tapped the cab driver on the shoulder to ask him something. When he did this the driver screamed, lost control of the car, nearly hit a bus, went up on the sidewalk, and stopped inches from a Starbuck's plate glass window. For a second everything went silent in the cab, then the unnerved driver said, "Look buddy, don't ever do that again. You scared me to death!" The passenger apologized and said he didn't realize that a little tap could startle him so much. The driver replied, "You're right. I'm sorry, really it's not your fault. Today is my first day driving a cab. I've been driving a hearse for 25 years."

Howard Thurman, the influential 20th century author, philosopher, theologian, and civil rights leader is quoted saying, "Don't ask yourself what the world needs. Ask yourself what makes you come alive, and go do that, because what the world needs is people who have come alive." It is our hope and prayer that *Give Me Your Heart: 40 Devotions for the Season of Lent* has helped your Lent and Easter come alive—and you along with them! Our world desperately needs Jesus, and who better to take Jesus to the world than you? So come alive, get out there, be you, use your gifts, and in the words of the apostle Paul, "May the God of hope fill you with all joy and peace as you trust in him, so that you may overflow with hope by the power of the Holy Spirit" (Romans 15:13).

Give Me Your Heart can be used for personal study and devotion as you move though the forty days of Lent towards the cross and empty tomb. It can also be used for small group study. We encourage you to gather once a week for approximately six weeks during the season of Lent, and use the following outline and questions to help focus and facilitate your group discussions when you gather together. It isn't necessary to go through all of the questions each week. What's most important is not information, but rather formation. So take your time, invite the Holy Spirit into your midst, and give God your heart. Here's an outline for a one-hour small group session.

Opening Prayer:

Open your time together with prayer. Someone may lead the group in prayer, or you can all pray together one of the prayers from the past week's devotions.

Questions for Discussion and Reflection:

Question 1 – What struck you about one of the devotions you read this past week? Did any of the statements, quotes, stories, or questions stir your soul?

Question 2 – Is there a Scripture that made an impact on you? What kind of impact?

Question 3 – Where did you see God at work this past week?

Question 4 – How did you resist God this past week?

Question 5 – How did you give God your heart this past week?

Question 6 – How have you served in the name of Christ this past week?

Question 7 – Have you shared your faith with anyone this past week? With whom, and how did you share your faith? What was their response?

Question 8 – Did any of the prayers this past week move you to a more meaningful relationship with God? If so, which one? How was your faith encouraged and/or strengthened?

Question 9 – Did you experience the movement of the Holy Spirit in your life this past week? If so, how? What difference does this experience make?

Question 10 – How do you expect to encounter God during this upcoming week?

Closing Prayer:

Close your time together with prayer. Someone may lead the group in prayer, or you can all pray together one of the prayers from the past week's devotions.

48604013R00056

Made in the USA
Lexington, KY
06 January 2016